Caring for Critters

Paul Mason

Author: Paul Mason
Editors: Kathy Middleton
Crystal Sikkens
Project coordinator: Kathy Middleton
Production coordinator: Ken Wright
Prepress technician: Margaret Amy Salter

Picture Credits:
Dreamstime: Sanja Baljkas: page 9; Miroslav Beneda: page 7; Dean Bertoncelj: page 19; Eric Isselée: pages 3, 16; Kenneth Lee: pages 1, 11; Xunbin Pan: page 20; Vladvitek: page 6
Shutterstock: cover, Joseph Calev: page 18; Matthew Cole: page 14; Steve Cukrov: page 21; EcoPrint: page 13; Eric Isselée: page 17; Cathy Keifer: pages 4, 10; Dr. Morley Read: page 15; Audrey Snider-Bell: page 12; Johan Swanepoel: page 5; yxm2008: page 8

Ask a parent or guardian for permission before purchasing any of the critters in this book to keep as a pet. Make sure if you do get a critter that it is kept in a safe and secure container.

Library and Archives Canada Cataloguing in Publication

Mason, Paul, 1967-
Caring for critters / Paul Mason.

(Crabtree connections)
Includes index.
ISBN 978-0-7787-7848-6 (bound).--ISBN 978-0-7787-7870-7 (pbk.)

1. Insects as pets--Juvenile literature. I. Title. II. Series: Crabtree connections

SF459.I5M38 2011 j638 C2011-900609-X

Library of Congress Cataloging-in-Publication Data

Mason, Paul, 1967-
Caring for critters / Paul Mason.
p. cm. -- (Crabtree connections)
Includes index.
ISBN 978-0-7787-7870-7 (pbk. : alk. paper) -- ISBN 978-0-7787-7848-6 (reinforced library binding : alk. paper)
1. Insects as pets--Juvenile literature. I. Title. II. Series.

SF459.I5M37 2011
638'.5--dc22

2011001348

Crabtree Publishing Company
www.crabtreebooks.com 1-800-387-7650

Printed in the U.S.A./072011/WO20110114

Published in Canada
Crabtree Publishing
616 Welland Ave.
St. Catharines, Ontario
L2M 5V6

Published in the United States
Crabtree Publishing
PMB 59051
350 Fifth Avenue, 59th Floor
New York, New York 10118

Contents

Critters are Cool

Do you want a pet? You could choose a pet dog or a cat or...

Bugs aren't boring!
If you want a really exciting pet, pick a **critter**.

How about keeping a **moth**?

On a roll

Dung beetles like rolling poop into balls. Gross!

Pretty pet

Ant Farm

Pet ants live in a special house called an ant farm. You can buy one from a pet shop.

Keep a perfect ant farm

1. Add a little water each day.
2. Add a drop of sugar water every week.

Feed your ants bits of apple and lettuce.

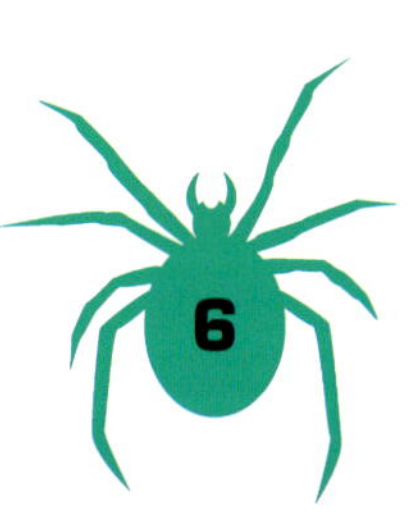

Two stomachs

Worker ants have an extra stomach. They store food in it to feed the colony's babies.

Feed me

Grasshopper

Grasshoppers make great pets and are easy to keep.

Make a hopper house

1. Put some soil in a small fish tank. Plant grass seed and spray with water.
2. Cover the top of the tank with **wire mesh.**

Don't let your grasshopper escape!

See me climb

Give your grasshopper plant stalks and twigs to climb. Hop to it!

Praying Mantis

Warning—this pet must be kept by itself. Put two together and they will fight to the death!

Make a mantis home

1. Fill a fish tank with leaves and twigs.
2. Cover the tank with wire mesh.

Feed your pet moths and flies—tasty!

Yum, yum

No squeezing

Don't pick it up. This pet's long, thin legs can easily break.

Scorpion

A scorpion isn't a pet you can hold because it has a sting in its tail!

Choose a scorpion

1. Pick a scorpion with a thin tail and large claws. Its **venom** is not harmful to humans.
2. Make sure your scorpion cannot climb the glass sides of its tank.

I'll sting!

Asleep in the deep freeze

Scorpions can survive being frozen. Scientists say they just **thaw** out and walk away!

Scorpions like to eat crickets.

Spider

If you get a pet spider, make sure it cannot escape. Imagine the scream if your mom saw it in the bathtub!

Keep a happy spider

1. Spiders love to spin **webs** on twigs and leaves. Put plenty in its home.
2. Give your spider a lot of flies to eat. Tasty!

Spider children

Some spiders have up to 800 babies.

Would you keep a **tarantula**!

Do I look annoyed?

Spiny Leaf Insect

If you want an amazing-looking pet, this is the one for you!

Handle carefully

1. To choose your pet, first you'll have to find it!
2. Don't hold this pet. It is easy to break its legs.

Leaf insects don't just look like leaves— they eat them too!

Girls can't fly
Only male spiny leaf insects have wings.
Leaf me alone!

Centipede

If you like to handle your pet, do not get a centipede. They have a sharp bite!

Looking after a centipede

1. Keep it in a **secure container**.
2. Never scare a centipede. It will bite!

I'll bite!

Centipedes have lots and lots of legs.

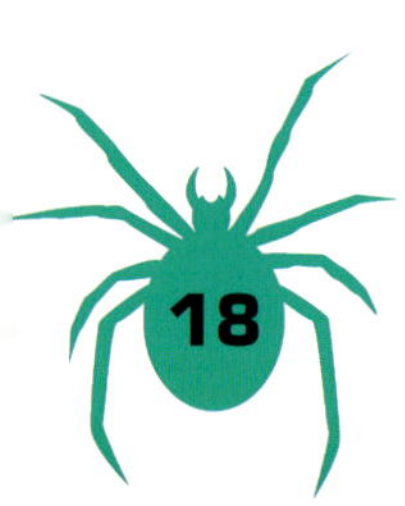

Up all night

Centipedes hunt for bugs at night.

Rhinoceros Beetle

A rhinoceros beetle can lift things that are 850 times heavier than itself! It's the world's strongest creature.

Keep a healthy rhino

1. Give it plenty of space. It loves to roam around.
2. Feed it rotting wood and fresh plants.

Gotta fly!

On the go

Rhinoceros beetles love climbing. Make sure your pet has a lot of twigs in its home.

Rhinoceros beetles are great flyers!

Glossary

colony A group of the same kind of animals living together

critter A fun word for bug, insect, or small creature

moths Insects a little like butterflies

secure container Holder or box from which a small creature cannot escape

tarantula Large, hairy, and poisonous spider

thaw When something melts after being frozen solid

venom Harmful poison

webs Sticky nets that spiders make from silk. Spiders eat flies and other insects that they catch in their webs.

wire mesh Net of wire threads with only small holes between them

Further Reading

Web Sites

Make your own critters at:
www.kenttrustweb.org.uk/kentict/content/games/minibeasts_v3.html

Find out more about the bugs and other animals in your backyard at:
www.backyardnature.net/animals.htm

Books

Living things in my back yard by Bobbie Kalman, Crabtree Publishing (2008).

The World of Insects series, Crabtree Publishing (2005-2006).

The ABCs of Insects by Bobbie Kalman, Crabtree Publishing (2009).

Backyard Encyclopedia by Rufus Bellamy, Crabtree Publishing (2011).

Backyard Bugs by Richard Ferguson, DK Publishing (2007).

Index